The Tale Jail

Written by
William Anthony

Illustrated by
Sasha Richards

Can you think of a place you never want to go?
I mean, like never ever?
For the baddies in kids' tales, that place is
The Tale Jail – a super-secure prison stuck
in the sea.

The Tale Jail

PHASE 5

/ea/

Level 8 – Purple

Helpful Hints for Reading at Home

The graphemes (written letters) and phonemes (units of sound) used throughout this series are aligned with Letters and Sounds. This offers a consistent approach to learning whether reading at home or in the classroom.

HERE IS A LIST OF PHONEMES FOR THIS PHASE OF LEARNING. AN EXAMPLE OF THE PRONUNCIATION CAN BE FOUND IN BRACKETS.

Phase 5			
ay (day)	ou (out)	ie (tie)	ea (eat)
oy (boy)	ir (girl)	ue (blue)	aw (saw)
wh (when)	ph (photo)	ew (new)	oe (toe)
au (Paul)	a_e (make)	e_e (these)	i_e (like)
o_e (home)	u_e (rule)		

Phase 5 Alternative Pronunciations of Graphemes			
a (hat, what)	e (bed, she)	i (fin, find)	o (hot, so, other)
u (but, unit)	c (cat, cent)	g (got, giant)	ow (cow, blow)
ie (tied, field)	ea (eat, bread)	er (farmer, herb)	ch (chin, school, chef)
y (yes, by, very)	ou (out, shoulder, could, you)		

HERE ARE SOME WORDS WHICH YOUR CHILD MAY FIND TRICKY.

Phase 5 Tricky Words			
oh	their	people	Mr
Mrs	looked	called	asked
could			

TOP TIPS FOR HELPING YOUR CHILD TO READ:

• Allow children time to break down unfamiliar words into units of sound and then encourage children to string these sounds together to create the word.

• Encourage your child to point out any focus phonics when they are used.

• Read through the book more than once to grow confidence.

• Ask simple questions about the text to assess understanding.

• Encourage children to use illustrations as prompts.

PHASE 5

/ea/

This book focuses on the grapheme /ea/ and is a purple level 8 book band.

Inside, The Three Bears were led to a cell. A man was leant on the wall, tapping an odd hook on the bars...

"Psst... Beasts! I'm Captain Hook. What did you do to end up in this dreadful place?"

"We were arrested for chasing a little girl called Goldilocks," said Mama Bear.
"But Goldilocks broke into our home to sneak around. She was never arrested," said Papa Bear with a huff.

"It is always the way," said Captain Hook.
"People think we are the bad ones."
The Three Bears nodded.
"Peter Pan cut off my hand, but it was me
who got put in jail."

"Look over there," said Hook. "That's the Witch from the woods. First, two little rascals called Hansel and Gretel tried to eat her home made of sweets. Then, they burned her when she was cooking!"

The Witch looked up.

"When I was cooking children," she admitted, "but there is nothing bad about that."

"There IS nothing bad about that!" agreed Captain Hook.

"The same happened with the Big Bad Wolf. He was testing the Three Little Pigs' homes to see if they could deal with bad weather."
"I was helping!" said the Wolf.
"He was helping!" agreed Captain Hook.

Captain Hook pointed to the Evil Queen.
"She just gave Snow White an apple."
"Snow White never told me she did not like poison!" squealed the Evil Queen.
"She never told her!" agreed Captain Hook.

"And that..." gulped Captain Hook, "that's Grandma. They say he tried to eat Little Red Riding Hood while pretending to be her grandma. It's all mean lies."

"No, no. I did do that," said Grandma as
he kept on weaving his yarn.
Captain Hook's jaw dropped.
"Oh," he said. "That's not great."

Captain Hook turned back to the Three Bears. "Do not sweat, we have a plan to break out of this unpleasant place. Meet us at breakfast in the morning."

The next day, the gang found each other in the canteen. The Three Bears sat next to the Big Bad Wolf and the Witch.

No one sat too close to Grandma after what she said the day before.

Captain Hook put a small bean on the bench. He said that a magic man from Cell Block B had told him it could reveal their way out of this dreadful prison.

So, that same night, the Evil Queen dug up some dirt in the yard and planted the bean. She gave it a splash of water and ran back inside.

One day later, the baddies were having their evening meal. Yet one person was missing – Captain Hook. The gang found him outside instead, looking up high into the clouds.

In front of him stood the biggest stem they had ever seen. It seemed to head past the clouds to a realm high in the heavens.

"That's our way out?" squealed Grandma. "We'll drop to our death!"

But then the stem swayed and shook.
A deep shout came from the top.

"Fee, fi, fo, fum! I'm going to kick Jack
up the bum!" it said.

A huge giant clambered down the stem.
"I want Jack!" screamed the Giant. "He stole
my chicken with the golden eggs!"
"We'll help you get him, but you need to help
us break out first," pleaded Captain Hook.

"Deal," agreed the Giant. They tried to shake hands, but with the Giant's size and Hook's... hook... it was not great.

Not that it mattered, it was never a real deal. These were baddies, after all.

The Giant reared up at the first wall and broke it with his head.

But the Giant did not stop. He broke down wall after wall after wall after wall with his huge head.

Captain Hook's jaw dropped for the
second time.
"Um... Time to break out, I suppose!"
he yelled.
The baddies ran down the tunnel of broken
prison walls that the Giant had carved.

Hee Hee Hee

"Run! Go, go, go!" screamed Papa Bear.
"Down the hill and to the coast!" yelled the
Big Bad Wolf.
The gang were not far in front of the cops.

Down on the coast, the gang looked for a way out.
Captain Hook's stressed face turned to a grin.
He spotted his pride and joy – a boat.
"Get on!" he yelled.

All was well... for a moment.
The Big Bad Wolf's fur was getting wet.
So were the Evil Queen's feet.
In the panic, the gang seemed to forget
they had a huge giant on the boat.

It was not long before the baddies were swimming to the nearest bit of land.
The gang looked at each other.
"Now what?" said Mama Bear. "We are stranded with no shelter or meals."

But then Grandma licked his lips and got out his fork and spoon.
"Don't mind these," muttered Grandma.
"All the better to eat you with!"

The baddies all ran away in fright and never saw each other again.

The Tale Jail

1. Who greeted the Three Bears as they were put into a cell?

2. Where did Captain Hook get a magic bean?
   (a)   Cell Block A
   (b)   Cell Block B
   (c)   Cell Block C

3. Who climbed down the giant stem?

4. If you were planning to break out of a jail, what would your plan be?

5. Why do people get taken to jail? Why is it important to be good?

BookLife
PUBLISHING

BookLife
Readers

© 2022 **BookLife Publishing Ltd.**
King's Lynn, Norfolk, PE30 4LS, UK

ISBN 978–1–80155–477–0

The Tale Jail
Written by William Anthony
Illustrated by Sasha Richards

An Introduction to BookLife Readers...

Our Readers have been specifically created in line with the London Institute of Education's approach to book banding and are phonetically decodable and ordered to support each phase of the Letters and Sounds document.

Each book has been created to provide the best possible reading and learning experience. Our aim is to share our love of books with children, providing both emerging readers and prolific page-turners with beautiful books that are guaranteed to provoke interest and learning, regardless of ability.

BOOK BAND GRADED using the Institute of Education's approach to levelling.

PHONETICALLY DECODABLE supporting each phase of Letters and Sounds.

EXERCISES AND QUESTIONS to offer reinforcement and to ascertain comprehension.

BEAUTIFULLY ILLUSTRATED to inspire and provoke engagement, providing a variety of styles for the reader to enjoy whilst reading through the series.

AUTHOR INSIGHT:
WILLIAM ANTHONY

William Anthony's involvement with children's education is quite extensive. He has written a vast array of titles for BookLife Publishing, across a wide range of subjects. William graduated from Cardiff University with a 1st Class BA (Hons) in Journalism, Media and Culture, creating an app and a TV series, among other things, during his time there.

William Anthony has also produced work for the Prince's Trust, a charity created by HRH The Prince of Wales, that helps young people with their professional future. He has created animated videos for a children's education company that works closely with the charity.

PHASE 5
/ea/

This book focuses on the grapheme /ea/ and is a purple level 8 book band.